This
Book Review Journal
Belongs To:

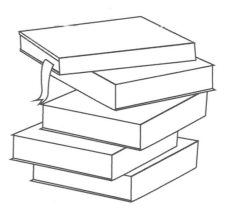

Title: _____

Author: _____

Genre: _____ Started: _____

Rating: ☆☆☆☆☆ Finished: _____

Favorite quotes:

_____
_____
_____
_____
_____
_____
_____
_____
_____
_____

My review:

_____
_____
_____
_____
_____
_____
_____
_____
_____
_____
_____

Title: _____

Author: _____

Genre: _____ Started: _____

Rating: ☆☆☆☆☆ Finished: _____

Favorite quotes:

_____
_____
_____
_____
_____
_____
_____
_____
_____

My review:

_____
_____
_____
_____
_____
_____
_____
_____
_____
_____
_____

Title: _____

Author: _____

Genre: _____ Started: _____

Rating: ☆☆☆☆☆ Finished: _____

Favorite quotes:

_____
_____
_____
_____
_____
_____
_____
_____
_____

My review:

_____
_____
_____
_____
_____
_____
_____
_____
_____
_____
_____

Title: _____

Author: _____

Genre: _____   Started: _____

Rating: ☆☆☆☆☆   Finished: _____

Favorite quotes:

_____
_____
_____
_____
_____
_____
_____
_____
_____

My review:

_____
_____
_____
_____
_____
_____
_____
_____
_____
_____
_____

Title: _____

Author: _____

Genre: _____   Started: _____

Rating: ☆☆☆☆☆   Finished: _____

Favorite quotes:

_____
_____
_____
_____
_____
_____
_____
_____
_____
_____

My review:

_____
_____
_____
_____
_____
_____
_____
_____
_____
_____
_____
_____

Title: _____

Author: _____

Genre: _____ Started: _____

Rating: ☆☆☆☆☆ Finished: _____

Favorite quotes:

_____
_____
_____
_____
_____
_____
_____
_____
_____
_____

My review:

_____
_____
_____
_____
_____
_____
_____
_____
_____
_____
_____
_____

Title: _____

Author: _____

Genre: _____ Started: _____

Rating: ☆☆☆☆☆ Finished: _____

Favorite quotes:

_____
_____
_____
_____
_____
_____
_____
_____
_____
_____

My review:

_____
_____
_____
_____
_____
_____
_____
_____
_____
_____
_____

Title: _____

Author: _____

Genre: _____ Started: _____

Rating: ☆☆☆☆☆ Finished: _____

Favorite quotes:

_____
_____
_____
_____
_____
_____
_____
_____
_____
_____

My review:

_____
_____
_____
_____
_____
_____
_____
_____
_____
_____
_____

Title: _____

Author: _____

Genre: _____   Started: _____

Rating: ☆☆☆☆☆   Finished: _____

Favorite quotes:

_____
_____
_____
_____
_____
_____
_____
_____
_____
_____

My review:

_____
_____
_____
_____
_____
_____
_____
_____
_____
_____
_____
_____

Title: _____

Author: _____

Genre: _____   Started: _____

Rating: ☆☆☆☆☆   Finished: _____

Favorite quotes:

_____
_____
_____
_____
_____
_____
_____
_____
_____
_____

My review:

_____
_____
_____
_____
_____
_____
_____
_____
_____
_____
_____
_____

Title: _____

Author: _____

Genre: _____   Started: _____

Rating: ☆☆☆☆☆   Finished: _____

Favorite quotes:

_____
_____
_____
_____
_____
_____
_____
_____
_____

My review:

_____
_____
_____
_____
_____
_____
_____
_____
_____
_____
_____

Title: _____

Author: _____

Genre: _____ Started: _____

Rating: ☆☆☆☆☆ Finished: _____

Favorite quotes:

_____
_____
_____
_____
_____
_____
_____
_____
_____
_____

My review:

_____
_____
_____
_____
_____
_____
_____
_____
_____
_____
_____
_____

Title: _____

Author: _____

Genre: _____   Started: _____

Rating: ☆☆☆☆☆   Finished: _____

Favorite quotes:

_____
_____
_____
_____
_____
_____
_____
_____
_____
_____

My review:

_____
_____
_____
_____
_____
_____
_____
_____
_____
_____
_____

Title: _____

Author: _____

Genre: _____ Started: _____

Rating: ☆☆☆☆☆ Finished: _____

Favorite quotes:

_____
_____
_____
_____
_____
_____
_____
_____
_____

My review:

_____
_____
_____
_____
_____
_____
_____
_____
_____
_____
_____

Title: _____

Author: _____

Genre: _____   Started: _____

Rating: ☆☆☆☆☆   Finished: _____

Favorite quotes:

_____
_____
_____
_____
_____
_____
_____
_____
_____

My review:

_____
_____
_____
_____
_____
_____
_____
_____
_____
_____
_____

Title: _____

Author: _____

Genre: _____ Started: _____

Rating: ☆☆☆☆☆ Finished: _____

Favorite quotes:

_____
_____
_____
_____
_____
_____
_____
_____
_____

My review:

_____
_____
_____
_____
_____
_____
_____
_____
_____
_____
_____

Title: _____

Author: _____

Genre: _____ Started: _____

Rating: ☆☆☆☆☆ Finished: _____

Favorite quotes:

_____
_____
_____
_____
_____
_____
_____
_____

My review:

_____
_____
_____
_____
_____
_____
_____
_____
_____
_____

Title: _____

Author: _____

Genre: _____   Started: _____

Rating: ☆☆☆☆☆   Finished: _____

Favorite quotes:

_____
_____
_____
_____
_____
_____
_____
_____
_____

My review:

_____
_____
_____
_____
_____
_____
_____
_____
_____
_____

Title: _____

Author: _____

Genre: _____ Started: _____

Rating: ☆☆☆☆☆ Finished: _____

Favorite quotes:

_____
_____
_____
_____
_____
_____
_____
_____
_____
_____

My review:

_____
_____
_____
_____
_____
_____
_____
_____
_____
_____
_____
_____

Title: _____

Author: _____

Genre: _____ Started: _____

Rating: ☆☆☆☆☆ Finished: _____

Favorite quotes:

_____
_____
_____
_____
_____
_____
_____
_____
_____
_____

My review:

_____
_____
_____
_____
_____
_____
_____
_____
_____
_____
_____
_____

Title: _____

Author: _____

Genre: _____   Started: _____

Rating: ☆☆☆☆☆   Finished: _____

Favorite quotes:

_____
_____
_____
_____
_____
_____
_____
_____

My review:

_____
_____
_____
_____
_____
_____
_____
_____
_____
_____

Title: _____

Author: _____

Genre: _____   Started: _____

Rating: ☆☆☆☆☆   Finished: _____

Favorite quotes:

_____
_____
_____
_____
_____
_____
_____
_____
_____

My review:

_____
_____
_____
_____
_____
_____
_____
_____
_____
_____
_____

Title: _____

Author: _____

Genre: _____   Started: _____

Rating: ☆☆☆☆☆   Finished: _____

Favorite quotes:

_____
_____
_____
_____
_____
_____
_____
_____
_____

My review:

_____
_____
_____
_____
_____
_____
_____
_____
_____
_____
_____

Title: _____

Author: _____

Genre: _____   Started: _____

Rating: ☆☆☆☆☆   Finished: _____

Favorite quotes:

_____
_____
_____
_____
_____
_____
_____
_____
_____

My review:

_____
_____
_____
_____
_____
_____
_____
_____
_____
_____

Title: _____

Author: _____

Genre: _____ Started: _____

Rating: ☆☆☆☆☆ Finished: _____

Favorite quotes:

_____
_____
_____
_____
_____
_____
_____
_____
_____

My review:

_____
_____
_____
_____
_____
_____
_____
_____
_____
_____
_____

Title: _____

Author: _____

Genre: _____ Started: _____

Rating: ☆☆☆☆☆ Finished: _____

Favorite quotes:

_____
_____
_____
_____
_____
_____
_____
_____
_____
_____

My review:

_____
_____
_____
_____
_____
_____
_____
_____
_____
_____
_____

Title: _____

Author: _____

Genre: _____   Started: _____

Rating: ☆☆☆☆☆   Finished: _____

Favorite quotes:

_____
_____
_____
_____
_____
_____
_____
_____
_____

My review:

_____
_____
_____
_____
_____
_____
_____
_____
_____
_____
_____

Title: _____

Author: _____

Genre: _____   Started: _____

Rating: ☆☆☆☆☆   Finished: _____

Favorite quotes:

_____
_____
_____
_____
_____
_____
_____
_____
_____

My review:

_____
_____
_____
_____
_____
_____
_____
_____
_____
_____

Title: _____

Author: _____

Genre: _____ Started: _____

Rating: ☆☆☆☆☆ Finished: _____

Favorite quotes:

_____
_____
_____
_____
_____
_____
_____
_____
_____

My review:

_____
_____
_____
_____
_____
_____
_____
_____
_____
_____

Title: _____

Author: _____

Genre: _____ Started: _____

Rating: ☆☆☆☆☆ Finished: _____

Favorite quotes:

_____
_____
_____
_____
_____
_____
_____
_____
_____
_____

My review:

_____
_____
_____
_____
_____
_____
_____
_____
_____
_____
_____

Title: _____

Author: _____

Genre: _____   Started: _____

Rating: ☆☆☆☆☆   Finished: _____

Favorite quotes:

_____
_____
_____
_____
_____
_____
_____
_____
_____

My review:

_____
_____
_____
_____
_____
_____
_____
_____
_____
_____

Title: _____

Author: _____

Genre: _____ Started: _____

Rating: ☆☆☆☆☆ Finished: _____

Favorite quotes:

_____
_____
_____
_____
_____
_____
_____
_____
_____
_____

My review:

_____
_____
_____
_____
_____
_____
_____
_____
_____
_____
_____

Title: _____

Author: _____

Genre: _____ Started: _____

Rating: ☆☆☆☆☆ Finished: _____

Favorite quotes:

_____
_____
_____
_____
_____
_____
_____
_____
_____

My review:

_____
_____
_____
_____
_____
_____
_____
_____
_____
_____
_____

Title: _____

Author: _____

Genre: _____ Started: _____

Rating: ☆☆☆☆☆ Finished: _____

Favorite quotes:

_____
_____
_____
_____
_____
_____
_____
_____
_____

My review:

_____
_____
_____
_____
_____
_____
_____
_____
_____
_____
_____

Title: _____

Author: _____

Genre: _____   Started: _____

Rating: ☆☆☆☆☆   Finished: _____

Favorite quotes:

_____
_____
_____
_____
_____
_____
_____
_____
_____
_____

My review:

_____
_____
_____
_____
_____
_____
_____
_____
_____
_____

Title: _____

Author: _____

Genre: _____ Started: _____

Rating: ☆☆☆☆☆ Finished: _____

Favorite quotes:

_____
_____
_____
_____
_____
_____
_____
_____
_____

My review:

_____
_____
_____
_____
_____
_____
_____
_____
_____
_____
_____

Title: _____

Author: _____

Genre: _____ Started: _____

Rating: ☆☆☆☆☆ Finished: _____

Favorite quotes:

_____
_____
_____
_____
_____
_____
_____
_____

My review:

_____
_____
_____
_____
_____
_____
_____
_____
_____
_____

Title: _____

Author: _____

Genre: _____ Started: _____

Rating: ☆☆☆☆☆ Finished: _____

Favorite quotes:

_____
_____
_____
_____
_____
_____
_____
_____
_____
_____

My review:

_____
_____
_____
_____
_____
_____
_____
_____
_____
_____
_____
_____

Title: _____

Author: _____

Genre: _____ Started: _____

Rating: ☆☆☆☆☆ Finished: _____

Favorite quotes:

_____
_____
_____
_____
_____
_____
_____
_____
_____
_____

My review:

_____
_____
_____
_____
_____
_____
_____
_____
_____
_____
_____

Title: _____

Author: _____

Genre: _____ Started: _____

Rating: ☆☆☆☆☆ Finished: _____

Favorite quotes:

_____
_____
_____
_____
_____
_____
_____
_____
_____

My review:

_____
_____
_____
_____
_____
_____
_____
_____
_____
_____
_____

Title: _____

Author: _____

Genre: _____   Started: _____

Rating: ☆☆☆☆☆   Finished: _____

Favorite quotes:

_____
_____
_____
_____
_____
_____
_____
_____
_____

My review:

_____
_____
_____
_____
_____
_____
_____
_____
_____
_____
_____

Title: _____

Author: _____

Genre: _____ Started: _____

Rating: ☆☆☆☆☆ Finished: _____

Favorite quotes:

_____
_____
_____
_____
_____
_____
_____
_____
_____

My review:

_____
_____
_____
_____
_____
_____
_____
_____
_____
_____
_____

Title: _____

Author: _____

Genre: _____ Started: _____

Rating: ☆☆☆☆☆ Finished: _____

Favorite quotes:

_____
_____
_____
_____
_____
_____
_____
_____
_____

My review:

_____
_____
_____
_____
_____
_____
_____
_____
_____
_____
_____

Title: _____

Author: _____

Genre: _____ Started: _____

Rating: ☆☆☆☆☆ Finished: _____

Favorite quotes:

_____
_____
_____
_____
_____
_____
_____
_____
_____

My review:

_____
_____
_____
_____
_____
_____
_____
_____
_____
_____

Title: _____

Author: _____

Genre: _____ Started: _____

Rating: ☆☆☆☆☆ Finished: _____

Favorite quotes:

_____
_____
_____
_____
_____
_____
_____
_____
_____
_____

My review:

_____
_____
_____
_____
_____
_____
_____
_____
_____
_____
_____

Title: _____

Author: _____

Genre: _____ Started: _____

Rating: ☆☆☆☆☆ Finished: _____

Favorite quotes:

_____
_____
_____
_____
_____
_____
_____
_____
_____

My review:

_____
_____
_____
_____
_____
_____
_____
_____
_____
_____
_____

Title: _____

Author: _____

Genre: _____ Started: _____

Rating: ☆☆☆☆☆ Finished: _____

Favorite quotes:

_____
_____
_____
_____
_____
_____
_____
_____
_____

My review:

_____
_____
_____
_____
_____
_____
_____
_____
_____
_____

Title: _____

Author: _____

Genre: _____   Started: _____

Rating: ☆☆☆☆☆   Finished: _____

Favorite quotes:

_____
_____
_____
_____
_____
_____
_____
_____
_____
_____

My review:

_____
_____
_____
_____
_____
_____
_____
_____
_____
_____
_____
_____

Title: _____

Author: _____

Genre: _____ Started: _____

Rating: ☆☆☆☆☆ Finished: _____

Favorite quotes:

_____
_____
_____
_____
_____
_____
_____
_____
_____

My review:

_____
_____
_____
_____
_____
_____
_____
_____
_____
_____
_____

Title: _____

Author: _____

Genre: _____ Started: _____

Rating: ☆☆☆☆☆ Finished: _____

Favorite quotes:

_____
_____
_____
_____
_____
_____
_____
_____
_____

My review:

_____
_____
_____
_____
_____
_____
_____
_____
_____
_____

Title: _____

Author: _____

Genre: _____   Started: _____

Rating: ☆☆☆☆☆   Finished: _____

Favorite quotes:

_____
_____
_____
_____
_____
_____
_____
_____
_____

My review:

_____
_____
_____
_____
_____
_____
_____
_____
_____
_____
_____

Title: _____

Author: _____

Genre: _____ Started: _____

Rating: ☆☆☆☆☆ Finished: _____

Favorite quotes:

_____
_____
_____
_____
_____
_____
_____
_____

My review:

_____
_____
_____
_____
_____
_____
_____
_____
_____
_____

Title: _____

Author: _____

Genre: _____ Started: _____

Rating: ☆☆☆☆☆ Finished: _____

Favorite quotes:

_____
_____
_____
_____
_____
_____
_____
_____
_____

My review:

_____
_____
_____
_____
_____
_____
_____
_____
_____
_____

Title: _____

Author: _____

Genre: _____   Started: _____

Rating: ☆☆☆☆☆   Finished: _____

Favorite quotes:

_____
_____
_____
_____
_____
_____
_____
_____
_____

My review:

_____
_____
_____
_____
_____
_____
_____
_____
_____
_____
_____

Title: _____

Author: _____

Genre: _____ Started: _____

Rating: ☆☆☆☆☆ Finished: _____

Favorite quotes:

_____
_____
_____
_____
_____
_____
_____
_____
_____

My review:

_____
_____
_____
_____
_____
_____
_____
_____
_____
_____
_____

Title: _____

Author: _____

Genre: _____ Started: _____

Rating: ☆☆☆☆☆ Finished: _____

Favorite quotes:

_____
_____
_____
_____
_____
_____
_____
_____
_____

My review:

_____
_____
_____
_____
_____
_____
_____
_____
_____
_____
_____

Title: _____

Author: _____

Genre: _____   Started: _____

Rating: ☆☆☆☆☆   Finished: _____

Favorite quotes:

_____
_____
_____
_____
_____
_____
_____
_____
_____

My review:

_____
_____
_____
_____
_____
_____
_____
_____
_____
_____
_____

Title: _____

Author: _____

Genre: _____ Started: _____

Rating: ☆☆☆☆☆ Finished: _____

Favorite quotes:

_____
_____
_____
_____
_____
_____
_____
_____
_____

My review:

_____
_____
_____
_____
_____
_____
_____
_____
_____
_____
_____

Title: _____

Author: _____

Genre: _____   Started: _____

Rating: ☆☆☆☆☆   Finished: _____

Favorite quotes:

_____
_____
_____
_____
_____
_____
_____
_____
_____

My review:

_____
_____
_____
_____
_____
_____
_____
_____
_____
_____
_____

Title: _____

Author: _____

Genre: _____ Started: _____

Rating: ☆☆☆☆☆ Finished: _____

Favorite quotes:

_____
_____
_____
_____
_____
_____
_____
_____
_____
_____

My review:

_____
_____
_____
_____
_____
_____
_____
_____
_____
_____
_____

Title: _____

Author: _____

Genre: _____   Started: _____

Rating: ☆☆☆☆☆   Finished: _____

Favorite quotes:

_____
_____
_____
_____
_____
_____
_____
_____
_____

My review:

_____
_____
_____
_____
_____
_____
_____
_____
_____
_____
_____

Title: _____

Author: _____

Genre: _____ Started: _____

Rating: ☆☆☆☆☆ Finished: _____

Favorite quotes:

_____
_____
_____
_____
_____
_____
_____
_____
_____
_____

My review:

_____
_____
_____
_____
_____
_____
_____
_____
_____
_____
_____

Title: _____

Author: _____

Genre: _____   Started: _____

Rating: ☆☆☆☆☆   Finished: _____

Favorite quotes:

_____

_____

_____

_____

_____

_____

_____

_____

_____

_____

My review:

_____

_____

_____

_____

_____

_____

_____

_____

_____

_____

_____

_____

Title: _____

Author: _____

Genre: _____   Started: _____

Rating: ☆☆☆☆☆   Finished: _____

Favorite quotes:

_____
_____
_____
_____
_____
_____
_____
_____
_____

My review:

_____
_____
_____
_____
_____
_____
_____
_____
_____
_____
_____

Title: _____

Author: _____

Genre: _____ Started: _____

Rating: ☆☆☆☆☆ Finished: _____

Favorite quotes:

_____
_____
_____
_____
_____
_____
_____
_____
_____

My review:

_____
_____
_____
_____
_____
_____
_____
_____
_____
_____
_____

Title: _____

Author: _____

Genre: _____ Started: _____

Rating: ☆☆☆☆☆ Finished: _____

Favorite quotes:

_____
_____
_____
_____
_____
_____
_____
_____
_____

My review:

_____
_____
_____
_____
_____
_____
_____
_____
_____
_____
_____

Title: _____

Author: _____

Genre: _____ Started: _____

Rating: ☆☆☆☆☆ Finished: _____

Favorite quotes:

_____
_____
_____
_____
_____
_____
_____
_____
_____

My review:

_____
_____
_____
_____
_____
_____
_____
_____
_____
_____
_____

Title: _____

Author: _____

Genre: _____ Started: _____

Rating: ☆☆☆☆☆ Finished: _____

Favorite quotes:

_____
_____
_____
_____
_____
_____
_____
_____
_____
_____

My review:

_____
_____
_____
_____
_____
_____
_____
_____
_____
_____
_____
_____

Title: _____

Author: _____

Genre: _____   Started: _____

Rating: ☆☆☆☆☆   Finished: _____

Favorite quotes:

_____
_____
_____
_____
_____
_____
_____
_____
_____
_____

My review:

_____
_____
_____
_____
_____
_____
_____
_____
_____
_____
_____
_____

Title: _____

Author: _____

Genre: _____ Started: _____

Rating: ☆☆☆☆☆ Finished: _____

Favorite quotes:

_____
_____
_____
_____
_____
_____
_____
_____
_____
_____

My review:

_____
_____
_____
_____
_____
_____
_____
_____
_____
_____
_____

Title: _____

Author: _____

Genre: _____ Started: _____

Rating: ☆☆☆☆☆ Finished: _____

Favorite quotes:

_____
_____
_____
_____
_____
_____
_____
_____
_____

My review:

_____
_____
_____
_____
_____
_____
_____
_____
_____
_____

Title: _____

Author: _____

Genre: _____   Started: _____

Rating: ☆☆☆☆☆   Finished: _____

Favorite quotes:

_____
_____
_____
_____
_____
_____
_____
_____
_____
_____

My review:

_____
_____
_____
_____
_____
_____
_____
_____
_____
_____
_____

Title: _____

Author: _____

Genre: _____ Started: _____

Rating: ☆☆☆☆☆ Finished: _____

Favorite quotes:

_____
_____
_____
_____
_____
_____
_____
_____
_____

My review:

_____
_____
_____
_____
_____
_____
_____
_____
_____
_____
_____

Title: _____

Author: _____

Genre: _____ Started: _____

Rating: ☆☆☆☆☆ Finished: _____

Favorite quotes:

_____
_____
_____
_____
_____
_____
_____
_____
_____

My review:

_____
_____
_____
_____
_____
_____
_____
_____
_____
_____
_____

Title: _____

Author: _____

Genre: _____ Started: _____

Rating: ☆☆☆☆☆ Finished: _____

Favorite quotes:

_____

_____

_____

_____

_____

_____

_____

_____

_____

My review:

_____

_____

_____

_____

_____

_____

_____

_____

_____

_____

_____

Title: _____

Author: _____

Genre: _____ Started: _____

Rating: ☆☆☆☆☆ Finished: _____

Favorite quotes:

_____
_____
_____
_____
_____
_____
_____
_____
_____

My review:

_____
_____
_____
_____
_____
_____
_____
_____
_____
_____
_____

Title: _____

Author: _____

Genre: _____   Started: _____

Rating: ☆☆☆☆☆   Finished: _____

Favorite quotes:

_____
_____
_____
_____
_____
_____
_____
_____
_____

My review:

_____
_____
_____
_____
_____
_____
_____
_____
_____
_____
_____

Title: _____

Author: _____

Genre: _____   Started: _____

Rating: ☆☆☆☆☆   Finished: _____

Favorite quotes:

_____
_____
_____
_____
_____
_____
_____
_____
_____

My review:

_____
_____
_____
_____
_____
_____
_____
_____
_____
_____
_____

Title: _____

Author: _____

Genre: _____   Started: _____

Rating: ☆☆☆☆☆   Finished: _____

Favorite quotes:

_____
_____
_____
_____
_____
_____
_____
_____

My review:

_____
_____
_____
_____
_____
_____
_____
_____
_____
_____

Title: _____

Author: _____

Genre: _____ Started: _____

Rating: ☆☆☆☆☆ Finished: _____

Favorite quotes:

_____
_____
_____
_____
_____
_____
_____
_____
_____
_____

My review:

_____
_____
_____
_____
_____
_____
_____
_____
_____
_____
_____
_____

Title: _____

Author: _____

Genre: _____ Started: _____

Rating: ☆☆☆☆☆ Finished: _____

Favorite quotes:

_____
_____
_____
_____
_____
_____
_____
_____
_____

My review:

_____
_____
_____
_____
_____
_____
_____
_____
_____
_____
_____

Title: _____

Author: _____

Genre: _____ Started: _____

Rating: ☆☆☆☆☆ Finished: _____

Favorite quotes:

_____
_____
_____
_____
_____
_____
_____
_____
_____

My review:

_____
_____
_____
_____
_____
_____
_____
_____
_____
_____
_____

Title: _____

Author: _____

Genre: _____   Started: _____

Rating: ☆☆☆☆☆   Finished: _____

Favorite quotes:

_____
_____
_____
_____
_____
_____
_____
_____
_____

My review:

_____
_____
_____
_____
_____
_____
_____
_____
_____
_____
_____

Title: _____

Author: _____

Genre: _____ Started: _____

Rating: ☆☆☆☆☆ Finished: _____

Favorite quotes:

_____
_____
_____
_____
_____
_____
_____
_____
_____
_____

My review:

_____
_____
_____
_____
_____
_____
_____
_____
_____
_____
_____

Title: _____

Author: _____

Genre: _____   Started: _____

Rating: ☆☆☆☆☆   Finished: _____

Favorite quotes:

_____
_____
_____
_____
_____
_____
_____
_____
_____
_____

My review:

_____
_____
_____
_____
_____
_____
_____
_____
_____
_____
_____
_____
_____

Title: _____

Author: _____

Genre: _____ Started: _____

Rating: ☆☆☆☆☆ Finished: _____

Favorite quotes:

_____
_____
_____
_____
_____
_____
_____
_____
_____
_____

My review:

_____
_____
_____
_____
_____
_____
_____
_____
_____
_____
_____
_____
_____

Title: _____

Author: _____

Genre: _____ Started: _____

Rating: ☆☆☆☆☆ Finished: _____

Favorite quotes:

_____
_____
_____
_____
_____
_____
_____
_____
_____

My review:

_____
_____
_____
_____
_____
_____
_____
_____
_____
_____
_____

Title: _____

Author: _____

Genre: _____ Started: _____

Rating: ☆☆☆☆☆ Finished: _____

Favorite quotes:

_____
_____
_____
_____
_____
_____
_____
_____
_____
_____

My review:

_____
_____
_____
_____
_____
_____
_____
_____
_____
_____
_____
_____

Title: _____

Author: _____

Genre: _____   Started: _____

Rating: ☆☆☆☆☆   Finished: _____

Favorite quotes:

_____
_____
_____
_____
_____
_____
_____
_____
_____
_____

My review:

_____
_____
_____
_____
_____
_____
_____
_____
_____
_____
_____
_____

Title: _____

Author: _____

Genre: _____ Started: _____

Rating: ☆☆☆☆☆ Finished: _____

Favorite quotes:

_____
_____
_____
_____
_____
_____
_____
_____
_____

My review:

_____
_____
_____
_____
_____
_____
_____
_____
_____
_____

Title: _____

Author: _____

Genre: _____   Started: _____

Rating: ☆☆☆☆☆   Finished: _____

Favorite quotes:

_____
_____
_____
_____
_____
_____
_____
_____
_____
_____

My review:

_____
_____
_____
_____
_____
_____
_____
_____
_____
_____
_____
_____

Title: _____

Author: _____

Genre: _____ Started: _____

Rating: ☆☆☆☆☆ Finished: _____

Favorite quotes:

_____
_____
_____
_____
_____
_____
_____
_____
_____

My review:

_____
_____
_____
_____
_____
_____
_____
_____
_____
_____
_____

Title: _____

Author: _____

Genre: _____ Started: _____

Rating: ☆☆☆☆☆ Finished: _____

Favorite quotes:

_____
_____
_____
_____
_____
_____
_____
_____

My review:

_____
_____
_____
_____
_____
_____
_____
_____
_____

Title: _____

Author: _____

Genre: _____ Started: _____

Rating: ☆☆☆☆☆ Finished: _____

Favorite quotes:

_____
_____
_____
_____
_____
_____
_____
_____
_____

My review:

_____
_____
_____
_____
_____
_____
_____
_____
_____
_____
_____

Title: _____

Author: _____

Genre: _____ Started: _____

Rating: ☆☆☆☆☆ Finished: _____

Favorite quotes:

_____
_____
_____
_____
_____
_____
_____
_____
_____
_____

My review:

_____
_____
_____
_____
_____
_____
_____
_____
_____
_____
_____
_____

Title: _____

Author: _____

Genre: _____ Started: _____

Rating: ☆☆☆☆☆ Finished: _____

Favorite quotes:

_____
_____
_____
_____
_____
_____
_____
_____
_____
_____

My review:

_____
_____
_____
_____
_____
_____
_____
_____
_____
_____
_____

Title: _____

Author: _____

Genre: _____ Started: _____

Rating: ☆☆☆☆☆ Finished: _____

Favorite quotes:

_____
_____
_____
_____
_____
_____
_____
_____
_____

My review:

_____
_____
_____
_____
_____
_____
_____
_____
_____
_____
_____

Made in the USA
Monee, IL
19 September 2022